Quarterback Dan Marino

FOOTBALL'S WEST COAST ERA

Wide receiver Jerry Rice

NFL SUPER BOWL STORIES

FOOTBALL'S WEST COAST ERA

(1985–1994)

JAMES BARRY

Defensive end Bruce Smith

CREATIVE EDUCATION / CREATIVE PAPERBACKS

Quarterback Joe Montana

Published by Creative Education and Creative Paperbacks
P.O. Box 227, Mankato, Minnesota 56002
Creative Education and Creative Paperbacks are imprints of The Creative Company
www.thecreativecompany.us

Design and production by Blue Design (www.bluedes.com)
Art direction by Graham Morgan
Edited by Kremena Spengler

Images by Associated Press/Four Seam Images, 16; Getty Images/Andy Hayt, 2, 7, 26–27, David Madison, cover, 3, Focus On Sport, 4–5, 6, 9, 11, 12, 22, 25, 29, 30, 32, George Gojkovich, 10, George Rose, 7, Jon Soohoo, 6, Otto Greule Jr, 7, 10, Owen C. Shaw, 28, RHONA WISE, 1, Rich Pilling/Diamond Images, 15, Rob Tringali/Sportschrome, 20, Robin Alam/Icon Sportswire, 6; NFL/Al Messerschmidt, 19, Don Lansu/WireImage.com, 14, Vernon Biever, 6
Every effort has been made to contact copyright holders for material reproduced in this book. Any omissions will be rectified in subsequent printings if notice is given to the publisher.

Library of Congress Cataloging-in-Publication Data
Names: Barry, James (Author of children's books), author.
Title: Football's west coast era (1985–1994) / James Barry.
Description: Mankato, Minnesota : Creative Education and Creative Paperbacks, [2026] | Series: Creative sports: NFL Super Bowl stories | Includes index. | Audience: Ages 8–12 | Audience: Grades 4–6 | Summary: "Joe Montana, Joe Gibbs, Emmitt Smith: Football's West Coast Era (1985–1994) was dominated by these names. Dramatic recaps introduce middle-grade readers to star NFL players from this era and ten exciting Super Bowls"– Provided by publisher.
Identifiers: LCCN 2024051459 (print) | LCCN 2024051460 (ebook) | ISBN 9798889896111 (library binding) | ISBN 9781682777770 (paperback) | ISBN 9798889896913 (ebook)
Subjects: LCSH: Football–Pacific Coast (America)–History–20th century–Juvenile literature. | Football players–Pacific Coast (America)–History–20th century–Juvenile literature. | Quarterbacks (Football)–Pacific Coast (America)–History–20th century–Juvenile literature. | National Football League–History–20th century–Juvenile literature.
Classification: LCC GV950.7 .B376 2026 (print) | LCC GV950.7 (ebook) | DDC 796.332/2–dc23/eng/20241122
LC record available at https://lccn.loc.gov/2024051459
LC ebook record available at https://lccn.loc.gov/2024051460

Printed in India

CONTENTS

SUPER BOWL LEGENDS

INTRODUCTION

It's the fourth quarter of Super Bowl XXIII (23). There are three minutes on the clock. The San Francisco 49ers have the ball on their own eight-yard line. They are down three points to the Cincinnati Bengals. But they have Joe Montana. Five completions later, the star quarterback has them in Cincinnati territory. He has no plans of settling for a field goal. He completes three straight passes. The last one is a 10-yard touchdown. It's Montana Magic! The 49ers complete a 92-yard scoring drive to take the game from the Bengals. They are Super Bowl champions.

Every team in the National Football League (NFL) wants to win the Super Bowl. It's the championship game between the best teams from each conference. In the 1980s, teams like the 49ers started using the passing game more and more. Quarterbacks like Montana became the game's most important players. Their legendary names and heart-pounding plays tell the story of football's "West Coast Era."

Wide receiver Jerry Rice (80), Super Bowl XXIII (23)

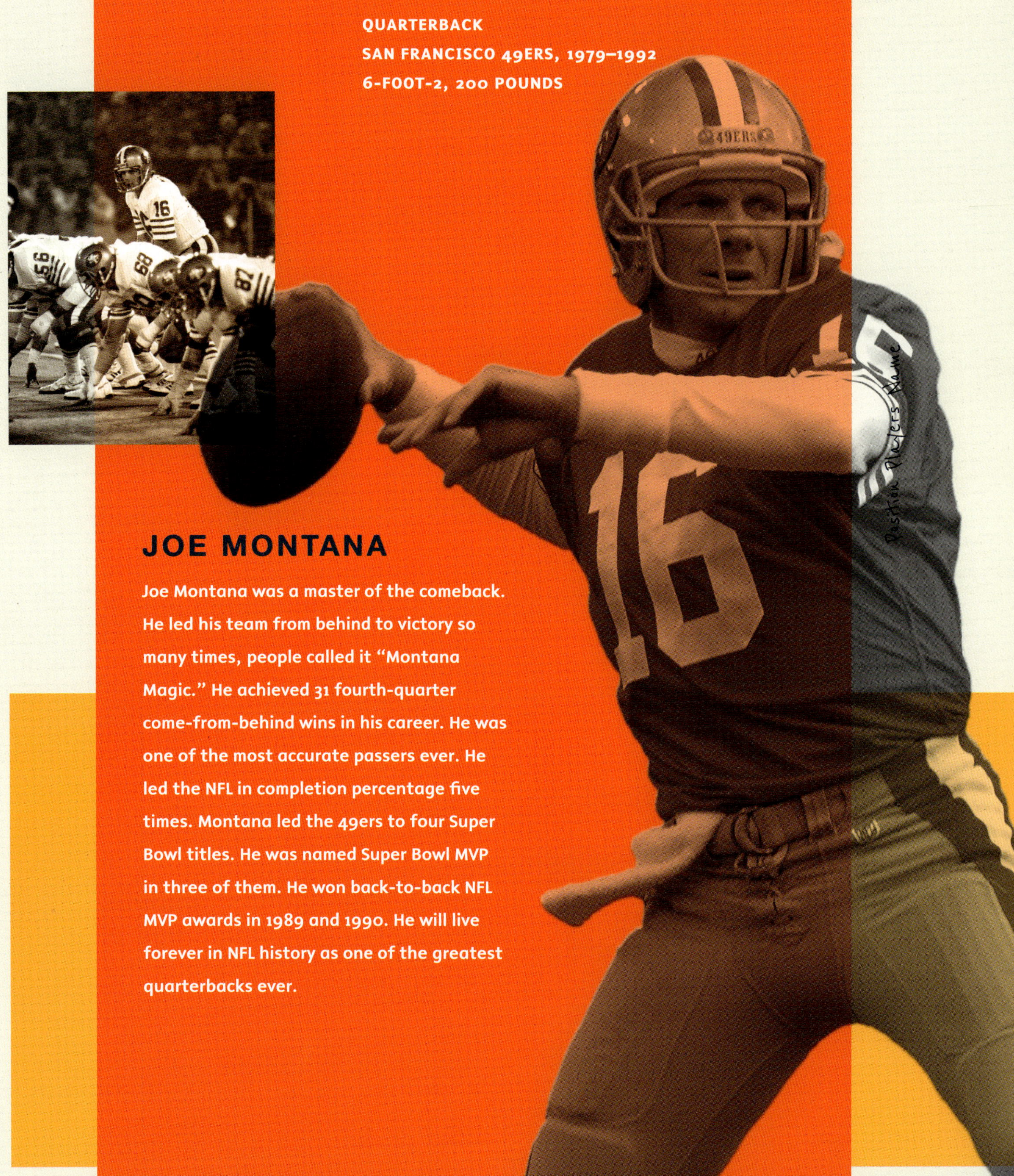

QUARTERBACK
SAN FRANCISCO 49ERS, 1979–1992
6-FOOT-2, 200 POUNDS

JOE MONTANA

Joe Montana was a master of the comeback. He led his team from behind to victory so many times, people called it “Montana Magic.” He achieved 31 fourth-quarter come-from-behind wins in his career. He was one of the most accurate passers ever. He led the NFL in completion percentage five times. Montana led the 49ers to four Super Bowl titles. He was named Super Bowl MVP in three of them. He won back-to-back NFL MVP awards in 1989 and 1990. He will live forever in NFL history as one of the greatest quarterbacks ever.

Running back Roger Craig

BIRTH OF THE WEST COAST OFFENSE

The San Francisco 49ers faced the Miami Dolphins in Super Bowl XIX (19). It was a battle between two great head coaches and two great quarterbacks. The Dolphins were led by coach Don Shula and quarterback Dan Marino. The 49ers were led by coach Bill Walsh and quarterback Joe Montana.

The Dolphins came into the game with a dominant offense. Marino set NFL records for completions, passing yards, and passing touchdowns in the regular season. He was the first quarterback to throw for 5,000 yards in a season. But the 49ers won 15 games in the regular season. They were the first team to do that. Their defense led the league in fewest points allowed. Montana had a great season of his own.

The two teams met at Stanford Stadium in Stanford, California. The first quarter was close. Montana completed a 33-yard touchdown pass to running back Carl Monroe. Marino answered with a touchdown drive of his own. In the second quarter, the 49ers took over. Their quick-hitting passing offense was

too much for Miami's weak defense. They scored 21 straight points. The Dolphins never recovered.

It was a historic night for Montana. He set the Super Bowl record with 331 passing yards. He also set the Super Bowl record for rushing yards by a quarterback, with 59. The Dolphins only ran for 29 yards as a team. Montana was named Super Bowl XIX (19) Most Valuable Player (MVP).

A FEW HISTORIC DEFENSES

The Chicago Bears faced the New England Patriots in Super Bowl XX (20). It was each team's first Super Bowl. New England was a surprise Super Bowl contender. The team reached the big game despite shaky play from its offense all year long. The Bears finished the regular season with 15 wins. They allowed the fewest yards and the fewest points in the NFL, and they led the league in forced turnovers. They outscored their opponents 456–198 in the regular season. The Bears were expected to win easily.

The two teams met at the Louisiana Superdome in New Orleans, Louisiana. The game got off to a surprise start. Bears running back Walter Payton fumbled less than a minute into the first quarter. The Patriots soon kicked a field goal to take a 3–0 lead. It was the quickest score in Super Bowl history. That would be all New England had to celebrate. The Bears led 23–3 at halftime.

Quarterback Jim McMahon

Linebacker Mike Singletary

Chicago quarterback Jim McMahon had a great game. He rushed for two touchdowns. But the star of the game was the defense. The unit was full of future Hall of Famers like Richard Dent and Mike Singletary. The Bears set Super Bowl records for sacks and fewest rushing yards allowed. They posted seven sacks and forced six turnovers. Chicago set Super Bowl records for points scored and margin of victory. The Bears won by a final score of 46–10. Defensive end Dent was named Super Bowl XX (20) MVP. To this day, the 1985 Bears are remembered as one of the greatest teams in NFL history.

Super Bowl XXI (21) was a matchup between the New York Giants and the Denver Broncos. The Giants completed a strong regular season with 14 wins. Their offense was led by quarterback Phil Simms and running back Joe Morris. Their defense was nicknamed the "Big Blue Wrecking Crew." It was led by fierce outside linebacker Lawrence Taylor. He led the league with 20.5 sacks in the season. He won his third Defensive Player of the Year award and his first MVP. The Broncos were carried to the Super Bowl almost single-handedly by star quarterback John Elway. Almost everyone expected the Giants to win.

The two teams met at the Rose Bowl in Pasadena, California. It was a close first half. The Broncos led 10–9 at halftime. Late in the second quarter, Elway was tackled in his own end zone by Giants defensive end George Martin. It was a safety. But those two points from the safety were the first of 26 straight points for the Giants. Elway had a great first half, but the Giants defense stepped up in

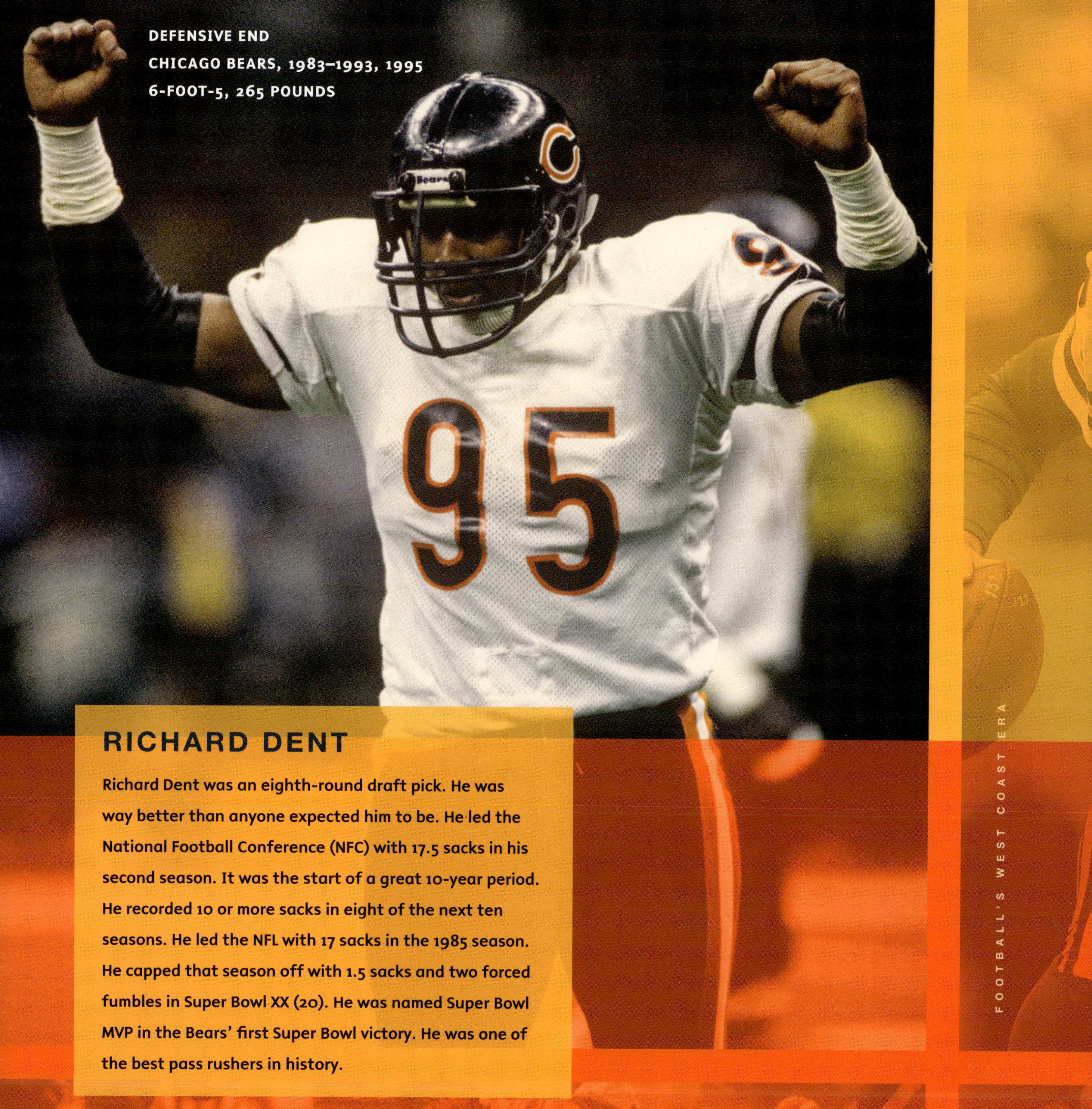

DEFENSIVE END
CHICAGO BEARS, 1983–1993, 1995
6-FOOT-5, 265 POUNDS

RICHARD DENT

Richard Dent was an eighth-round draft pick. He was way better than anyone expected him to be. He led the National Football Conference (NFC) with 17.5 sacks in his second season. It was the start of a great 10-year period. He recorded 10 or more sacks in eight of the next ten seasons. He led the NFL with 17 sacks in the 1985 season. He capped that season off with 1.5 sacks and two forced fumbles in Super Bowl XX (20). He was named Super Bowl MVP in the Bears' first Super Bowl victory. He was one of the best pass rushers in history.

LINEBACKER
NEW YORK GIANTS
1981–1993
6-FOOT-3, 237 POUNDS

LAWRENCE TAYLOR

Lawrence Taylor was known as "L.T." He changed the outside linebacker position. Instead of reacting to the offense, he attacked the offense. He could get past offensive linemen with speed and strength. Many outside linebackers have since tried to play like him. He was dominant as soon as he entered the NFL. Taylor won the Defensive Player of the Year award as a rookie. He went on to win it two more times. He was named first-team All-Pro in each of his first nine seasons. Taylor won the NFL MVP award in 1986. He won two Super Bowls with the Giants.

the second half, and Simms put together a historic night passing. He completed 22 of his 25 pass attempts for a Super Bowl record completion percentage. He finished the game with 268 passing yards and 3 touchdowns.

A late touchdown pass from Elway made the final score closer than the game was. The Giants won by a score of 39–20. Simms was named Super Bowl XXI (21) MVP. The Giants won their first Super Bowl.

THE QUARTERBACKS TAKE OVER AGAIN

The Broncos returned to face the Washington Redskins in Super Bowl XXII (22). Once again Elway carried the Broncos to the big game. He posted an MVP regular season with nearly 3,200 yards passing and 23 total touchdowns. The Redskins were counting on their backup quarterback, Doug Williams. He replaced the struggling Jay Schroeder. He was the first Black quarterback to start in a Super Bowl.

The two teams met at Jack Murphy Stadium in San Diego, California. Elway started the game with a bang. He completed a 56-yard touchdown pass on Denver's first play of the game. The Broncos led 10–0 after another scoring drive a few minutes later. The Broncos were moving the ball, and the Redskins weren't. Things changed in the second quarter. Williams started it off with an

80-yard touchdown pass to wide receiver Ricky Sanders. Then he threw another touchdown pass a few minutes later. Then things got crazy.

The Redskins scored 35 straight points in the second quarter. Williams threw four touchdown passes. It was a Super Bowl record. The Redskins led 35–10 at halftime, and the Broncos never scored again. Washington won by a final score of 42–10.

Williams made history. He was named Super Bowl XXII (22) MVP. It was the second Super Bowl victory for Redskins head coach Joe Gibbs. It was the second straight blowout Super Bowl loss for the Broncos.

The San Francisco 49ers faced the Cincinnati Bengals in Super Bowl XXIII (23). The 49ers had a great offense again led by Joe Montana. His favorite targets were wide receiver Jerry Rice and running back Roger Craig. The Bengals were led by quarterback Boomer Esiason. He was the NFL MVP. He threw for 3,572 yards and 28 touchdowns in the regular season.

The two teams met at Joe Robbie Stadium in Miami, Florida. The score was tied 3–3 at halftime. The first big play came late in the third quarter. The 49ers had just made a field goal to tie the game again at 6–6. Then Bengals running back Stanford Jennings returned the kickoff for a 93-yard touchdown. Three Montana completions and 85 yards later, the game was tied again. The score was 13–13 in the fourth quarter.

Esiason led the Bengals on a long scoring drive. It ended with a 40-yard field goal from kicker Jim Breech. Cincinnati led 16–13, with under four minutes left. It

Quarterback Doug Williams

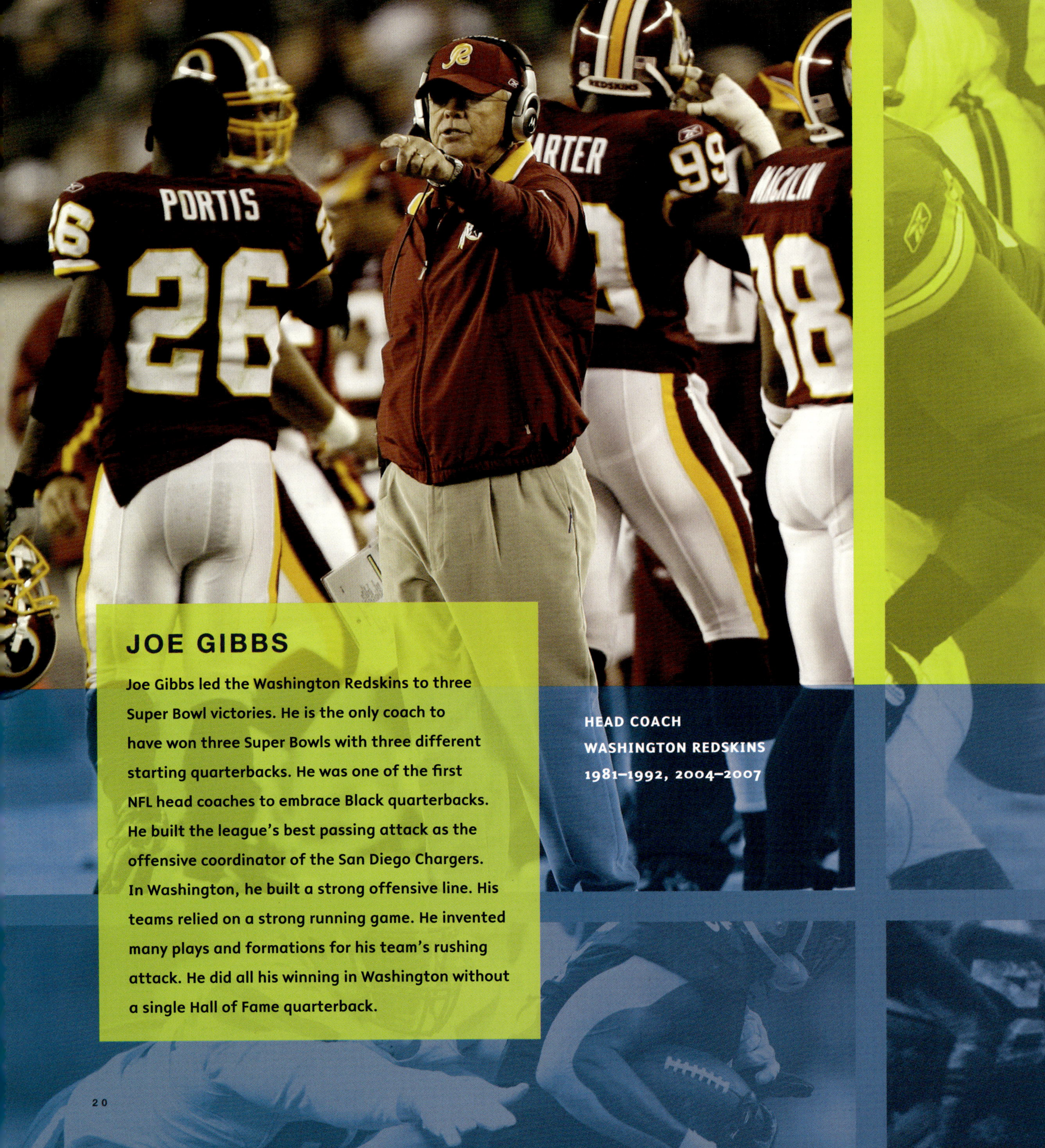

JOE GIBBS

Joe Gibbs led the Washington Redskins to three Super Bowl victories. He is the only coach to have won three Super Bowls with three different starting quarterbacks. He was one of the first NFL head coaches to embrace Black quarterbacks. He built the league's best passing attack as the offensive coordinator of the San Diego Chargers. In Washington, he built a strong offensive line. His teams relied on a strong running game. He invented many plays and formations for his team's rushing attack. He did all his winning in Washington without a single Hall of Fame quarterback.

HEAD COACH
WASHINGTON REDSKINS
1981–1992, 2004–2007

was time for Montana to work his magic. He completed passes to Rice and Craig all the way down the field. He led them on a 92-yard scoring drive that ended in a touchdown pass to wide receiver John Taylor. Kicker Mike Cofer made the extra point. The 49ers took the lead with 34 seconds left. They won Super Bowl XXIII (23) by a final score of 20–16. San Francisco won their third Super Bowl in as many tries.

The 49ers returned to defend their title against the Broncos in Super Bowl XXIV (24). San Francisco finished the season with a league-best 14 wins. Montana was still dominant. He won the NFL MVP and the Offensive Player of the Year award. The 49ers' offense led the NFL in total yards and in scoring. The Broncos were playing in their fourth Super Bowl. They were trying to avoid losing for the fourth time. Elway had a poor regular season. But he seemed to be playing his best football in the playoffs.

The two teams met at the Louisiana Superdome. San Francisco struck first. Montana completed a 20-yard touchdown pass to Rice on the team's first possession. The Broncos responded with a field goal. Then Montana threw another touchdown pass in the first quarter. It was all 49ers from there on. The score was 41-3 in the third quarter.

Montana didn't even play for most of the fourth quarter. He still finished with 297 passing yards and five touchdowns. Elway completed only 10 of 26 attempts and threw two interceptions. The 49ers won by a final score of 55–10. Montana and the team set too many Super Bowl records to list. It was the most points scored by a team and the biggest margin of victory in Super Bowl history. Montana set the record for touchdown passes in a Super Bowl. He won his third Super Bowl MVP.

ROLLE
87
69
67
11
PARKER
74
14

WIDE RIGHT AND DOWN BAD

Super Bowl XXV (25) was a matchup between the New York Giants and the Buffalo Bills. Again New York was led by its defense. The Giants allowed the fewest points in the NFL. Their offense lost starting quarterback Phil Simms to injury. He was replaced by backup Jeff Hostetler. The Bills also had a strong defense led by defensive end Bruce Smith. He recorded 19 sacks and won the Defensive Player of the Year. But Buffalo was especially known for its fast-paced offense. The Bills were led by quarterback Jim Kelly. He finished the season as the NFL's top-rated passer.

It was a battle of two different styles. The Bills led the NFL in points scored. The Giants led the NFL in fewest points allowed. The two teams met at Tampa Stadium in Tampa, Florida. The first quarter was slow and low-scoring. The first touchdown of the game came early in the second quarter. Buffalo finished an 80-yard scoring drive with a handoff to running back Don Smith. The Bills led 10–3. Hostetler led the Giants on an 87-yard touchdown drive to end the first half. Buffalo led 12–10 at halftime.

It was a close game for all four quarters. The Giants finally took the lead, with eight minutes left in the fourth quarter. A field goal from kicker Matt Bahr put

Kicker Scott Norwood (11)

them up 20–19. They held the lead until Buffalo got the ball, with two minutes left. It came down to a field goal from Buffalo kicker Scott Norwood, with eight seconds left. Norwood missed it wide to the right. Bills fans and players were left in disappointment. The Giants were Super Bowl XXV (25) champions.

The Bills returned to Super Bowl XXVI (26) to face the Redskins. It was a battle of two great offenses. The Redskins offense was led by quarterback Mark Rypien. He led the conference in passing yards and passing touchdowns. The Bills were still running their fast-paced "no-huddle" offense. Quarterback Jim Kelly was still leading the charge. But the Redskins had one of the best defenses in the league. The Bills had one of the worst.

The two teams met at the Metrodome in Minneapolis, Minnesota. Neither team scored in the first quarter. Both quarterbacks threw interceptions. Things changed in the second quarter—for Washington, at least. Rypien threw a touchdown pass to running back Earnest Byner. Then Kelly threw another interception. Rypien led Washington on another touchdown drive. The Redskins led 17–0 at halftime.

It was a rough game for Kelly. He started the second half with a third interception. One play later, the Redskins were up 24–0. The Bills cut the lead down to 14 in the third quarter. But Rypien answered with a 30-yard touchdown pass to wide receiver Gary Clark. Rypien had a strong game; Kelly had one of his worst. The Bills' quarterback turned it over six times in the game. Rypien was named Super Bowl XXVI (26) MVP. The Redskins were Super Bowl champions.

The Bills weren't done yet. They returned to a third straight Super Bowl to face the Cowboys in Super Bowl XXVII (27). Once again they had one of the NFL's best offenses. But people still expected the Cowboys to win. It was a different Dallas

Quarterback Mark Rypien

Riddell
Wilson

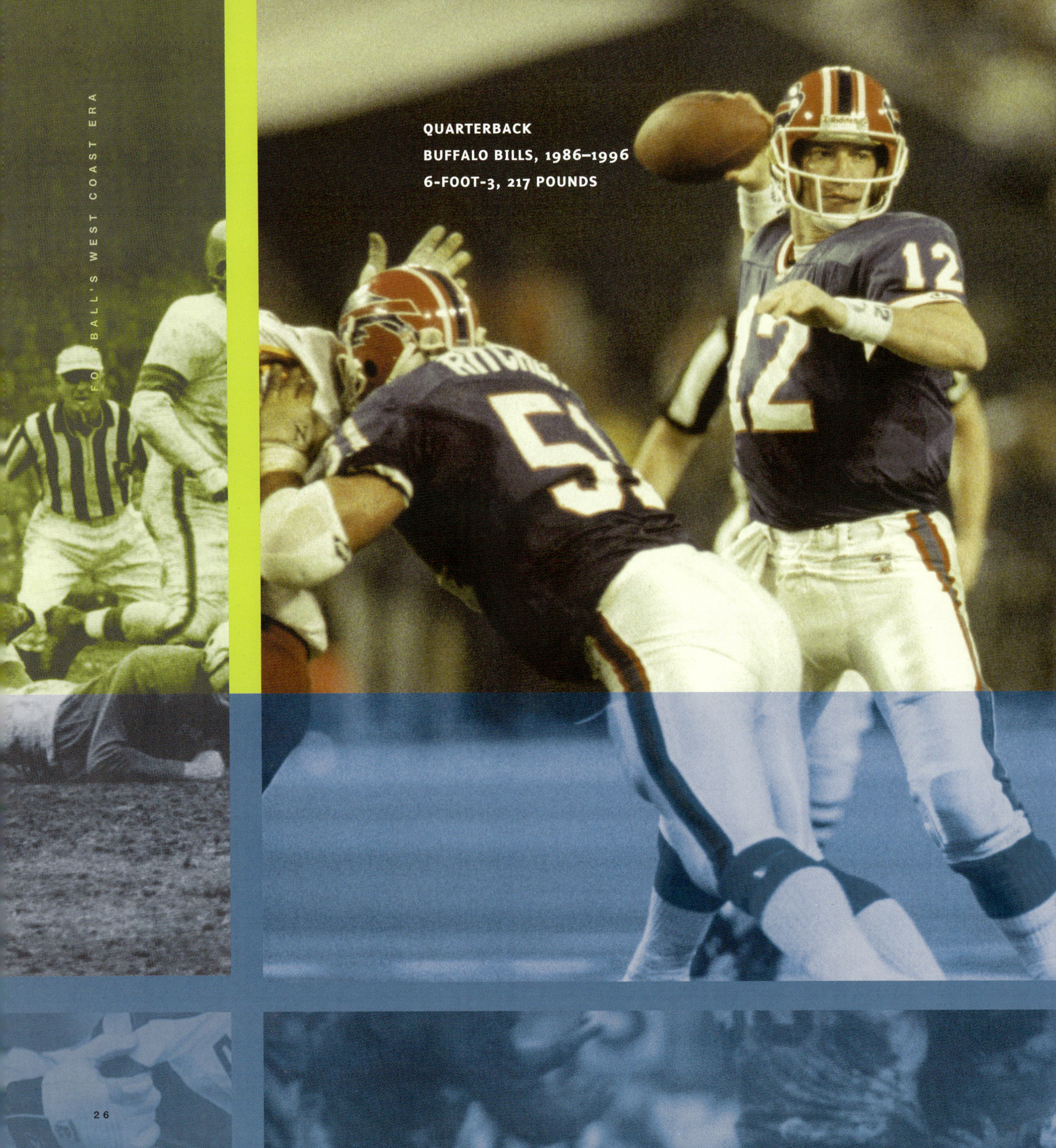

QUARTERBACK
BUFFALO BILLS, 1986–1996
6-FOOT-3, 217 POUNDS

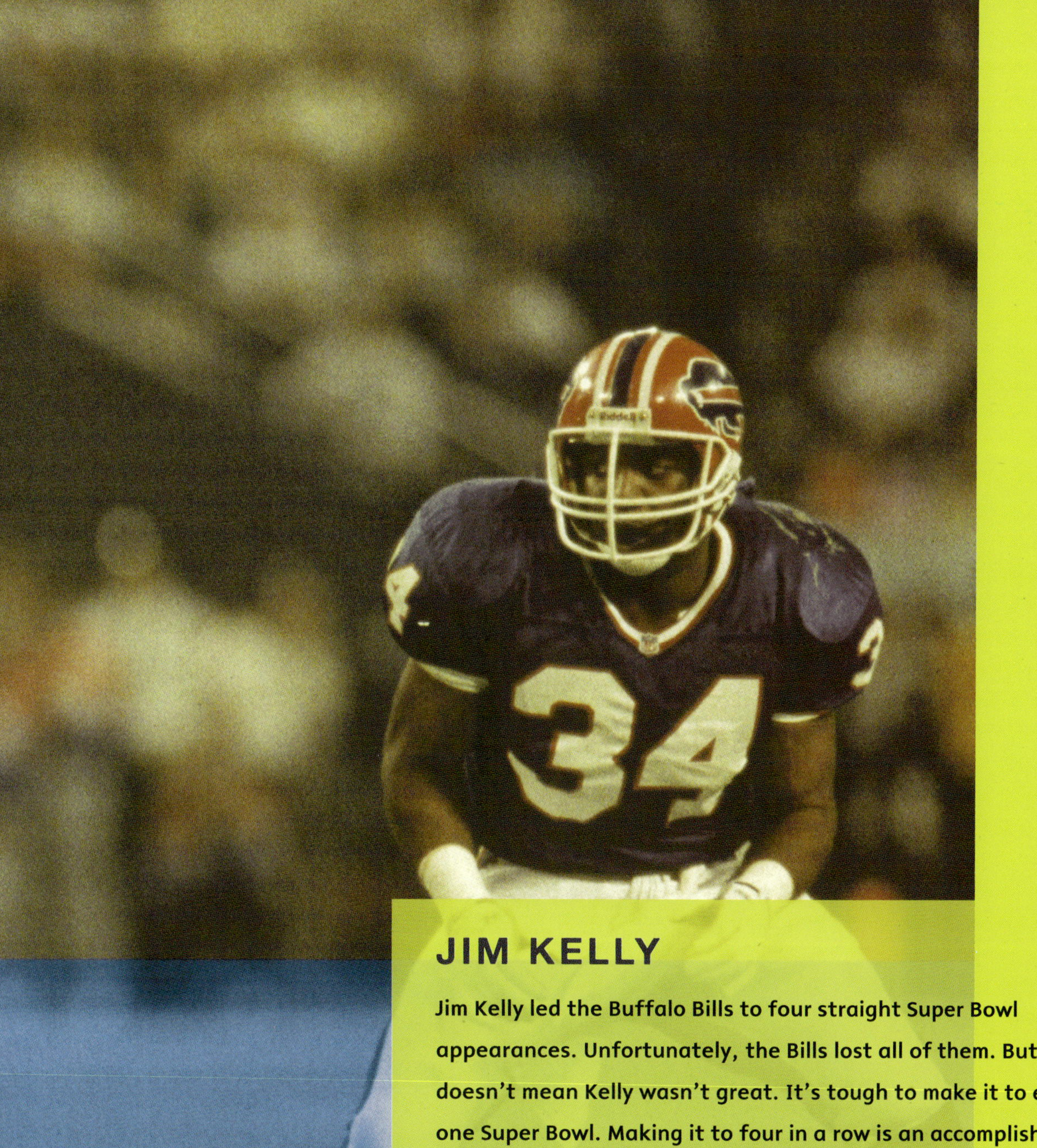

JIM KELLY

Jim Kelly led the Buffalo Bills to four straight Super Bowl appearances. Unfortunately, the Bills lost all of them. But that doesn't mean Kelly wasn't great. It's tough to make it to even one Super Bowl. Making it to four in a row is an accomplishment in itself. He was Buffalo's first-round pick in 1983. But he chose to sign with the Houston Gamblers of the United States Football League (USFL). In two seasons with the Gamblers, he threw for 9,842 yards and 83 touchdowns. Then the USFL folded, and Kelly finally joined the Bills. He became Buffalo's greatest quarterback.

Running back Thurman Thomas

team in this Super Bowl, led by head coach Jimmy Johnson. The Cowboys had one of the league's best defenses, and its best offensive line. The offense was led by quarterback Troy Aikman and running back Emmitt Smith.

The two teams met at the Rose Bowl. Thurman Thomas ran for a two-yard touchdown to give Buffalo the lead. Later in the first quarter, Kelly threw his first interception of the game. Aikman made the Bills pay for it. He completed a 23-yard touchdown pass to tie the game. Kelly turned the ball over on his very next play. He was sacked and lost a fumble near his own endzone. It was recovered and returned for a Dallas touchdown.

Buffalo didn't stop turning the ball over. Kelly threw another interception in the second quarter. Aikman threw for two more touchdowns. Star wide receiver

EMMITT SMITH

Emmitt Smith is the NFL's all-time leader in rushing yards and rushing touchdowns. He won three Super Bowls with the Cowboys. He won NFL MVP and Super Bowl MVP in the same season in 1993. He posted 11 straight seasons of 1,000 or more yards rushing. That's still an NFL record. Running backs take more hits than any other position. It's a tough position that usually leads to shorter careers. Smith set the all-time standard for running back longevity. He was great for more than a decade. He's still atop the NFL record books.

RUNNING BACK
DALLAS COWBOYS, 1990–2002
5-FOOT-9, 221 POUNDS

Michael Irvin caught both. Kelly left the game with an injury. His replacement was Frank Reich. He threw an interception on his first possession. Dallas led 28–10 at halftime. The Bills set a Super Bowl record by turning the ball over nine times. The Cowboys won by a final score of 52–17. Aikman threw for 273 yards and four touchdowns. He was named Super Bowl XXVII (27) MVP.

Believe it or not, the Bills still weren't done. They made their fourth Super Bowl in a row and faced the Cowboys again in Super Bowl XXVIII (28). It was the only time the same two teams met in two straight Super Bowls. Kelly became the first quarterback to start in four straight Super Bowls. Dallas running back Smith won his third rushing title and his first NFL MVP. Aikman was still great.

The two teams met at the Georgia Dome in Atlanta, Georgia. It seemed like the Bills were finally on their way to a Super Bowl victory. A Thomas rushing touchdown in the second quarter gave Buffalo a 10–6 lead. An Aikman interception near the end of the first half led to a Buffalo field goal. The Bills led 13–6 at halftime.

Buffalo started with the ball in the second half. Then Thomas lost a fumble. It was recovered by Cowboys safety James Washington. He returned it 48 yards for a touchdown. The game was tied 13–13. And just like that, the Bills lost their momentum. Smith took control of the game for the Cowboys. He scored two touchdowns. Kelly and the Bills' offense couldn't move the ball anymore. Dallas won the game by a final score of 30–13. Smith was named Super Bowl XXVIII (28) MVP. The Cowboys won back-to-back Super Bowls. The Bills lost four in a row.

With this dominant performance by Smith, football's West Coast Era came to an end. Defensive coaches would soon catch up to the passing offenses that beat them. Another era of great defense was on the way.

Quarterback Troy Aikman

INDEX